For Dominic

First published Great Britain in 2010

ISBN: 978-0-9562692-9-4

Blue Stevens photographs on pages 73, 77, 78 © Guildford Museum 2007

Blue Stevens Publishing

BLUE ❦ STEVENS
www.bluestevens.com

Printed in Lithuania

GUILDFORD

PHOTOGRAPHY BY BLUE STEVENS

Blue Stevens Publishing

BLUE STEVENS

www.bluestevens.com

FOREWORD

I was born in Albury, a village in the North Downs just outside Guildford, and from an early age developed a love of the local area. I have spent most of my life living and working in and around Guildford, and when I discovered the joys of digital photography I delighted in setting out to capture my favourite places on camera.

I hope the pictures in this book reveal my vision of Guildford in all its seasons and at all times of day, with just the amount of narrative to put the images in context.

I have had to be selective, and to leave out many features that would form a comprehensive coverage of the town, but I believe that I have caught the essence of Guildford, its dynamism, colour and rich heritage, and the beauty of the surrounding countryside.

Blue Stevens

ACKNOWLEDGEMENTS

I am delighted to have this opportunity to thank my family and friends for their unstinting support, encouragement and enthusiasm, and for all they have done in helping to bring about this exciting project. In particular to my sister Jo and her husband, Graham, my brother Toby, and John Twining, for giving so generously of his time in researching and writing the narrative for the photographs.

I would also like to thank those who kindly gave me permission to take and use photographs of buildings and artefacts: Anthony Richmond, Master of Abbot's Hospital; Phil Thompson, Regional Manager of Bateman's Opticians (a subsidiary of Vision Express); Jill Draper and Rowland Sidwell, Heritage Department, Guildford Borough Council; Tony Lyddon, Administrator, Guildford Cathedral; The Rector and Church Wardens of Holy Trinity and St Mary's, Guildford; William Pye, Sculptor of 'Narcissus'; Guildford Spectrum; John Twining, for his 1822 Map of Guildford; University of Surrey.

My thanks go also to Gintare Ralyte in Lithuania, who arranged and managed the printing of this book with such care and attention, and who took every step to ensure its successful completion.

And finally, a very special thank you to Dominic, whose encouragement started me on the path to photography, and whose patience, help and practical support have been my rock and inspiration.

CONTENTS

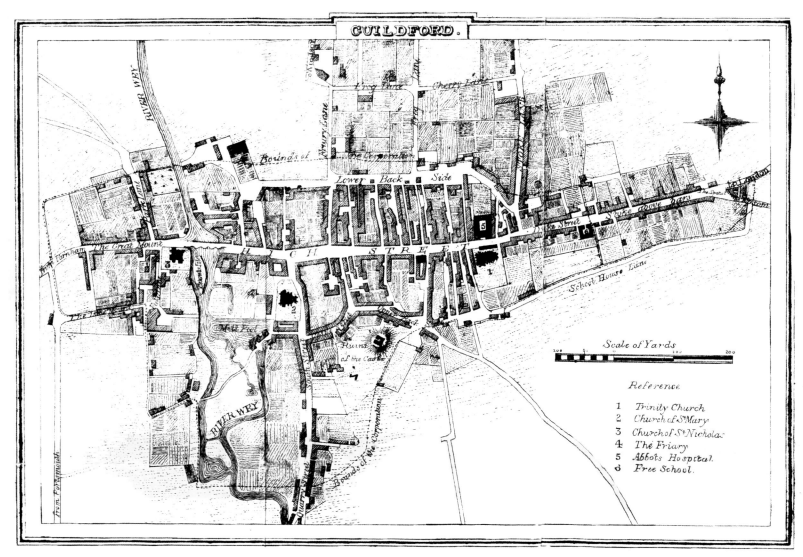

GUILDFORD.

Scale of Yards

Reference

1 Trinity Church
2 Church of St Mary
3 Church of St Nicholas
4 The Friary
5 Abbots Hospital
6 Free School

J. Greig Lithogr Islington

Published February 1st 1822 by Messrs Longman & Co Paternoster Row

THE RIVER WEY

THE RIVER WEY

River Crossings

Guildford has grown where the River Wey flows through a gap in the North Downs. Indeed the town gets its name from the golden ford, a river crossing made golden by sands on the river bank or in the river bed, or perhaps by the golden flowers growing nearby.

In fact there was more than one ford. One was where the town bridge now is, with steep hillsides east and west of the river crossing and with St Nicolas church on one side of the river and the High Street on the other. This is the nucleus from which the town grew.

The medieval stone bridge had to be replaced in 1900 by an iron bridge when a flood swept timber from a nearby yard against its piers, which broke. In the 1980s the structure was deemed unsafe and was replaced with the present bridge, now for pedestrians only.

The other ford was at the foot of St Catherine's hill, some half mile upstream from the town bridge. This ford, still with its sandy beaches and with low lying meadows on the east bank, was replaced by a ferry in about 1760 when the river was dredged, and eventually by a foot bridge in 1980.

Town Bridge; St Nicholas Church from Town Bridge; St Catherine's Bridge

< The River Wey

Millmead Footbridge

St Catherine's Weir

Early Morning at St Catherine's

The Wey Navigation

In 1651 an Act of Parliament enabled the building of the Wey Navigation, which linked Guildford to the Thames at Weybridge. Its twelve locks were completed by 1653 and wharfs were constructed downstream of the town bridge. At first the Navigation was badly run and its owner had to sell his shares and was imprisoned for debt. But in the 1670s new management made it profitable and Guildford prosperous. From 1671 the Guildford Corporation levied a toll of one penny per ton of merchandise and used it to support the poor of the town and the maintenance of its streets.

The Wey Navigation predated the English canal boom by the best part of a century. In 1761 the Godalming Navigation extended the navigable waterway four miles upstream; in 1796 the Navigation was linked to the national canal network via the Basingstoke Canal and in 1813 to the south coast via the Wey and Arun Canal. Barges were built at Dapdune Wharf, some of 80-90 tons capacity.

The cargoes were mainly bulk agricultural produce and building materials, profitable as London grew, with coal as a return cargo. Gunpowder was also transported from the mills at Chilworth, initially through Guildford town to the town wharf, but after the Godalming Navigation was opened to a safer wharf at Shalford. Commerce on the Wey is commemorated by the statue of a bargeman and the reconstruction of the treadwheel crane which, powered by two men, lifted heavy loads out of and into barges.

Stoke Lock

Dapdune Wharf

Dapdune Wharf

Millmead Lock

Millmead Lock

The Bargeman

Treadwheel Crane

St Catherine's Lock

Riverside Buildings

Like the river itself and its Navigations, riverside buildings have undergone a change of use or, in the case of some pubs, a change of name. The Weyside Inn, pictured opposite, was formerly The Jolly Farmer.

Guildford's professional theatre, the Yvonne Arnaud, was completed in 1961 on the site of an iron foundry, demolished 20 years earlier. The town mill is on a site where corn was milled from the middle ages to the 1890s. It has been converted into a small theatre, the Mill Studio, and is a scenery workshop and store for the Yvonne Arnaud.

An electrical generating plant was built in 1913 on the site of the old Militia barracks. It was unused from the 1920s but has now been adapted to form the Electric Theatre, a venue for amateur groups, comedians and international singers and dancers.

Further downstream is Stoke Mill, a nineteenth century paper mill. The Mill has been converted into offices and is currently the Head Office for the Surrey Advertiser group of newspapers, covering the Guildford area and beyond.

The Weyside Inn

Town Mill

Yvonne Arnaud Theatre

Electric Theatre

Stoke Mill

Recreation

The Wey Navigation was privately owned, but in 1964 the then owner, Harry Stevens, donated it to the National Trust. In 1969 the Trust acquired the Godalming Navigation and now maintains the whole waterway from Weybridge to Godalming as a major resource for recreation. It is used by rowing, kayaking and fishing clubs and is open under licence to boat owners. Narrow boats and rowing boats can be hired at Guildford Boathouse, which also offers river trips to Godalming. The Guildford Boat Festival with decorated narrow boats, and home made rafts racing for charity, is held in July.

The towpath is open to walkers and cyclists along the full nineteen and a half miles from Godalming to Weybridge.

Guildford Boathouse

Narrow Boats on the River Wey

Guildford Raft Race

Kayaks on the River Wey

THE
NORTH DOWNS WAY

THE NORTH DOWNS WAY

The North Downs Way is one of the 15 National Trails of England and Wales, designated by Natural England, which advised the government on the environment.   This trail runs 153 miles from Farnham to Dover, mostly using ancient tracks and where possible following the tops of the Downs.   It offers a traffic-free route for walkers, cyclists and horse riders.

The North Downs Way should not be confused with the Pilgrim's Way. In Victorian times an officer of the Ordnance Survey gave this name to some of the ancient tracks from Winchester to Canterbury.   The Pilgrim's Way was given spurious authenticity by inclusion on Ordnance Survey maps. The tracks it follows tend to run along the lower slopes of the downs and in many cases have been incorporated into the road system. In some places the North Downs Way and the Pilgrim's Way converge.

From Farnham the North Downs Way runs eastward along the chalk ridge known as the Hogs Back. Where the River Wey cuts through the chalk the trail descends to St Catherine's Hill with its ancient chapel, consecrated in 1329.   From 1308 a major fair was held at St Catherine's, originally for five days in the autumn. In Victorian times the fair declined, only running for two days, and ceased altogether from 1914, while the chapel fell into disuse and is now a ruin.

St Catherine's Chapel

< View from the Hogs Back

The North Downs Way crosses the River Wey below St Catherine's Hill, and runs across Shalford meadows before climbing the hillside to Chantries Wood, owned by the Guildford Borough Council since 1930. It then passes by the foot of Pewley Downs, given to Guildford by the Friary Brewery in 1920 as a memorial to those who died in World War I. The chalk downs had provided good grazing for sheep in medieval and Tudor times and Guildford's prosperity at that time was based on the manufacture of woollen cloth.

A number of ancient tracks, including the North Downs Way and the Pilgrim's Way, converge on St Martha's Hill. At the top of the hill stands St Martha's church, a Victorian reconstruction of a much earlier ruin, partly damaged by a great explosion in the Chilworth gunpowder mills in 1763. According to the Editor of the 1911 Victoria County History St Martha's was "an object lesson of the mischievous results of fanciful restoration". However it is a favourite spot for walkers, offering outstanding views of the Surrey Hills, and many visitors today find the church and its setting attractive and it is a popular venue for weddings.

The Chantries, early morning sunlight

The Chantries, view towards Chilworth

Pewley Downs

Spring Lambs

Pewley Downs

Grinding Stones, Old Gunpowder Mill, Chilworth

Footpath to St Martha's

St Martha's Church

Pilgrims Way, St Martha's >

Further along the North Downs Way from St Martha's is Newlands Corner, a famous beauty spot with panoramic views of the Surrey hills. In 1926 the novelist Agatha Christie, whose husband was being unfaithful, staged her disappearance by leaving her Morris Cowley car on a grassy slope, triggering a large but unsuccessful hunt for her. After 11 days she was discovered at a hotel in Harrogate.

At the foot of the downs near Newlands Corner is the Silent Pool, haunted by the ghost of Emma. According to legend, she was a woodcutter's daughter who was bathing naked in the lake when a horseman rode by, said to have been Prince John, Regent of England. To preserve her modesty she retreated further into the lake as he tried to entice her out of the water. She got into difficulties and her brother, working nearby, heard her cries for help. Unfortunately he also was not a good swimmer. The horseman rode off, leaving both brother and sister to drown. There is indeed a ghostly atmosphere about the Silent Pool.

The North Downs Way turns south to Hackhurst Downs, designated as a Site of Special Scientific Interest and a local Nature Reserve because of the amount of chalk grassland fauna and flora. The North Downs Way then continues eastwards towards Dover.

The Silent Pool

Newlands Corner

The Silent Pool

< Newlands Corner

The Silent Pool

A winter's afternoon, Hackhurst Downs

44

EARLY GUILDFORD

EARLY GUILDFORD

Quarry Street

Saxon Guildford was a settlement along what is now Quarry Street, which later became the coach road to Portsmouth.

Guildford was not included in the Burghal Hidage, a list of the fortified towns and forts built by King Alfred and his son Edward the Elder (died 924) to resist the Viking invasions; the nearest burgh was at Eashing, some five miles from Guildford. However Guildford was sufficiently important to have had a mint by 975.

St Mary's Church

The only Saxon building now remaining in Guildford is the tower of St Mary's church in Quarry Street, which has been dated as being as early as mid-10th century. It is likely that the stone tower replaced an earlier wooden one. The transepts are early Norman. The chancels and side chapels are higher than the nave because St Mary's was built on a hill.

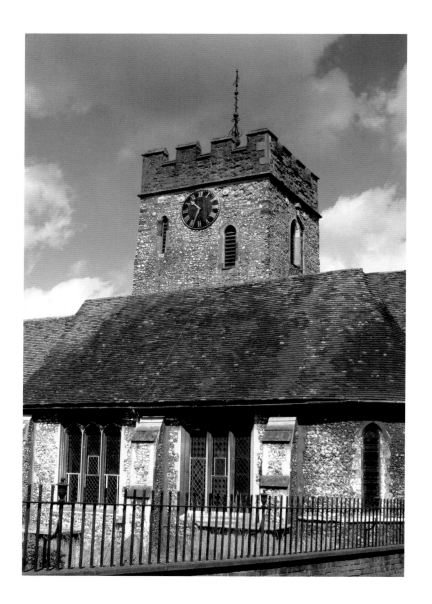

St Mary's Church

< Quarry Street

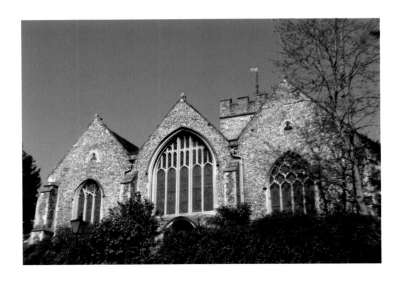

St Mary's Church

The Castle Arch is thought to have been built in 1256 under the supervision of Henry VIII's Master Mason, John of Gloucester, as the main entrance to the castle complex.

Next to the Arch, Guildford Museum is housed in a building thought to be part medieval, but largely adapted and rebuilt by the Carter family in about 1639.

Castle Arch

Guildford Museum and Castle Arch

Guildford Castle

Over the centuries Guildford Castle has had many roles. It was built by the Normans as a fortification guarding the river crossing, but the only time it saw action was in 1216, when it surrendered tamely to the French army invited by the barons to oppose King John. Later in the thirteenth century it was rebuilt as a royal palace for Henry III, his wife Queen Eleanor of Provence and their son, the future Edward I.

From 1202 to the 16th century the Keep was the County Gaol for Surrey and Sussex. In 1611 King James I sold the castle to a local merchant, Francis Carter, who tried unsuccessfully to make a home in the Keep. Later uses have included a cockpit, a source of building material as the town grew, and a private boys' school.

The Borough Council bought the remains of the castle and grounds for £2,200 in 1885, and laid out a public park around the Keep, which has now been carefully restored.

The adjacent bowing green was bought by the Borough Council separately from the castle for £2,050. In 1921 the town War Memorial was built next to the bowling green. It holds the names of 440 Guildfordians who died in World War I. In 1995 202 names were added of those who died in World War II. The War Memorial is the focal point for the annual Armistice Day service.

Castle Grounds >

Outer Wall, Guildford Castle

War Memorial

Bowling Green

The High Street

THE HIGH STREET

Guildford High Street is not only the historic commercial and administrative heart of the town but also, with its granite sets (laid in 1868), protruding clock and the green back drop of the Mount, is itself the centrepiece of Guildford. Many important buildings line the High Street; quite a few (unlike the riverside buildings) are still used for the same purpose for which they were originally designed.

The Royal Grammar School

In the early 16th century a wealthy London grocer, Robert Beckingham, left property to a charity for the maintenance of a free school in Guildford. The Charities Act 1547 required all property owned by charities to revert to the King. The Mayor and citizens of Guildford petitioned the young Edward VI for a charter and an income for the school, and these were granted. In 1555 the corporation bought land just inside the town boundary and building of the school started in 1557, although it was not completed until 1586.

In a court case in 1598 one of the witnesses claimed that he and his fellow scholars at the Royal Grammar School "did runne and play there at Creckett and other plaies" on the plot of land in dispute. This is said to be the first written reference to the game of cricket.

Royal Grammar School

Abbot's Hospital and the Cloth Hall

George Abbot was born in Guildford in 1562, the son of a cloth worker. He was educated at the Royal Grammar School and Balliol College. George Abbott had an illustrious scholastic career at Oxford University and was one of the Oxford scholars who translated much of the New Testament (the Gospels, Acts of the Apostles and Revelation) from Greek for the Authorised Version of the Bible. In 1609 he was made Bishop of Lichfield and Coventry, in 1610 Bishop of London and then, from 1611 until his death in 1633, Archbishop of Canterbury. His statue stands at the junction of High Street and North Street and his tomb is in Holy Trinity church.

In 1619 Gorge Abbot founded and endowed the Hospital of the Blessed Trinity (usually known as Abbot's Hospital) as an almshouse for elderly poor who had been born, or had lived for many years, in Guildford. In the original almshouse eight single poor 'sisters' and 12 poor 'brethren' were housed in brick built blocks round a central rectangular courtyard. Modernisation in 1986 also enabled seven couples to be housed. The entrance from the High Street is a massive brick gatehouse with domed turrets at each of its four corners.

In the 17th Century the wool trade was in general decline, partly due to the replacement of woollen cloth by other textiles. In 1629 George Abbot built the Cloth Hall behind Abbot's Hospital. He hoped to revive the cloth trade by providing a 'manufactory' where local people were paid to be trained in the weaving of linen. This venture was not a success and in 1656 the Cloth Hall was converted into a poorhouse, later a school and now a shop.

Cloth Hall

Abbot's Hospital

Coat of Arms above entrance, Abbot's Hospital

Inner Courtyard, Abbot's Hospital >

The Three Pigeons

The Three Pigeons has been a pub since 1755, although beer had been sold there from 1646. The building was badly damaged by fire in 1916 and was rebuilt with a mock Jacobean front.

Holy Trinity Church

In April 1740 the tower of the medieval church of the Holy Trinity collapsed, destroying the whole church except a small chantry chapel. Although Holy Trinity was the town church it took over 20 years before the church was rebuilt, in red brick, on the original site opposite Abbot's Hospital. A flight of steps leading from the High Street to the north door provides a ceremonial entrance for civic processions.

The Three Pigeons

Holy Trinity Church

Holy Trinity Church

Holy Trinity Church

Guildford House

Further down the High Street is Guildford House, built for John Child, a Guildford lawyer, in 1660. Over the years Guildford House has had several uses and since 1959 has been the town's art gallery, with over 100,000 visitors a year. The house and its contents give a good idea of how wealthy Guildfordians would have lived in the 17th and 18th centuries. In 2010 the Borough Council decided to locate the Guildford Tourist Information Centre in Guildford House.

Tunsgate Arch

Since the 17th century sacks of corn had been stored under cover in the Tun Inn opposite the Guildhall. By 1818 this was inadequate and so the Inn was demolished and replaced by a grand Corn Exchange in Tuscan style, built by public subscription. At first the County Assizes were also held in the building but it was very noisy. In 1860 the judge became so angry about the noise that he cleared the public from the court. When the Sheriff of Guildford protested that clearing the court was unlawful the judge fined him £500. Complaints about noise continued even when the Assizes were moved to the County and Borough Hall in North Street in 1861. As Guildford failed to provide reasonable court facilities, in 1930 the Assizes were transferred to Kingston.

Tunsgate Arch is now the impressive southern entrance to the middle of the High Street.

Guildford House

Guildford House, Stained Glass Window

Tunsgate Arch

Tunsgate Flower Market

The Guildhall

The Guildhall was originally a Tudor building to which, in 1683, a Council Chamber and a balcony over the High Street were added to the first floor, with a bell tower above. The original bell (reputed to have come from St Martha's Church) cracked, was replaced and is now kept in the Guildhall lobby. Guildford's Coat of Arms, featuring a castle and two woolsacks, sits over a fireplace by the Council Chamber.

Until the 20th century the Guildhall was where the Mayor and councillors met and where a court was held. The Council last met in the Guildhall in 1931 and courts continued until 2000. The Guildhall is still used for ceremonial occasions.

The Clock

In the seventeenth century the Guild Merchant controlled the right to trade in Guildford. The story goes that John Aylward, who was not a native of Guildford, was refused permission to trade as a clock maker by the Guild Merchant. However, when the Guildhall was being extended in 1683 he donated the clock which projects over the High Street and as a reward was given permission to trade in the town. Whether or not this story is true the Guildhall clock is now a defining image of Guildford.

Guildhall and Clock

Council Chamber >

Guildhall: Guildford's Coat of Arms; courtroom; original bell

Guildhall Clock >

The Angel Hotel

Guildford is about halfway between London and the major naval base of Portsmouth. From the mid-17th to early 19th century Britain was constantly engaged in naval wars and Guildford was a natural stopping place for coach traffic. At the start of the period roads were so bad that the London to Portsmouth journey often took 16 hours, and coach passengers would frequently stay overnight at one of Guildford's fine coaching inns.

In the mid-18th century the introduction of turnpike trusts to run toll roads led to great improvements in road surfaces and the London to Portsmouth journey was reduced to nine hours. But the inns remained as posting houses (which hired horses), and provided livery stables for their customers. In the early 19th century there were ten coaches per day each way through Guildford, between them perhaps carrying some 200 passengers. But in the 1840s the railway (cheaper, faster and less uncomfortable) replaced the coaches.

The Angel Posting House is the only remaining coaching inn in Guildford. While it dates from at least the time of Henry VIII, it has a Regency front. The archway leads to Angel gate, now a courtyard with an outdoor café area. Still in place is the hoist for lifting hay up to a loft above the stables.

Angel Gate

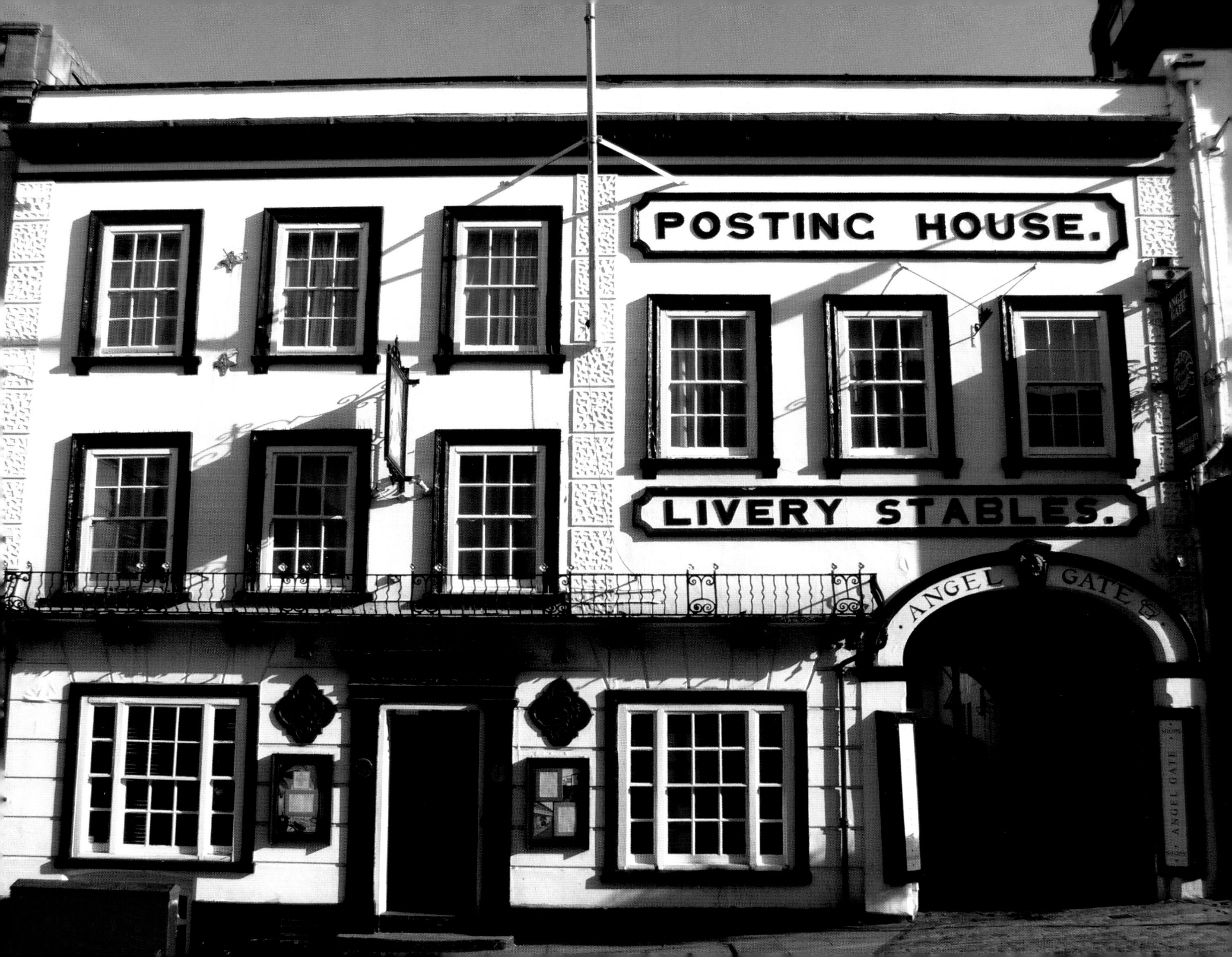
POSTING HOUSE.
LIVERY STABLES.
ANGEL GATE
ANGEL GATE

Activities

Although it is on a steep hillside, Guildford High Street provides space for many different activities, including parades and civic processions.

Historically markets were held in the High Street. The livestock market was moved to North Street in 1865, and other markets were also moved to North Street later in the 19th Century. Since 1973, when the High Street was pedestrianised, street markets have been revived, but not for livestock. Farmers' markets are held monthly and craft markets several times a year.

Other activities have included a children's Carnival and Morris Dancing.

At Christmas time the High Street is full of shoppers, and after dark it is ablaze with lights.

Street Market, Guildford High Street

Carnival, High Street

Morris Dancers on May Day, High Street

Christmas Lights, High Street

OPEN SPACES

Open Spaces

Guildford is fortunate to have green open spaces surrounding the town and pushing into the centre. Some have been pictured in earlier chapters: the Wey, Chantry Woods and Pewley Downs, the castle grounds and bowling green.

But there are others. Behind the south end of Quarry Street is Racks Close, where dyed cloths were hung to dry when the wool trade brought the town prosperity. It is still a green open space.

To the south of the town centre, in the river valley, are Shalford meadows where in the summer families can picnic to the sound of music and where pageants have been held to commemorate great events. Also down by the riverside is the Woodbridge Road cricket ground where club and county cricket matches are played.

Another venue for events is Stoke Park, close to the town centre, which was bought by the council in 1925 for £42,500; all attempts to recoup the purchase price by developing for housing were defeated. The Spectrum leisure centre was built on the north side of the park, where a proposal in the 1970s to provide a site for Surrey County Council was thwarted by the House of Lords. Stoke Park is also home to the annual Surrey County show and to the musical festival Guilfest. Stoke Park has sports pitches and a children's playground but also quiet corners like the boating pond, with a bridge leading to a small central island.

The west of the town is dominated by the Mount, at the end of the ridge of the Downs, providing the back drop to the High Street and a paradise for tobogganers in the snow.

In the east Merrow Downs have remained an open space despite a multiplicity of uses. In the 18th and 19th centuries there was a race course across the downs, but it lost out to Ascot and Epsom and the last race was held in 1870. Guildford's golf course has been on Merrow Downs since 1886. During World War II a prisoner of war camp was sited there and the huts were used for temporary housing for several years after the war. Merrow Downs are now recognised as rare chalk downland, so this open space is likely to be preserved.

< The Mount

Rack's Close

Shalford Meadows

Cattle on Shalford Meadows

93

Guildford Cricket Ground, Woodbridge Road

Guildford Spectrum

Guildford County Show, Stoke Park

Boating Pond, Stoke Park

Merrow Downs

Toboganning on the Mount >

Guildford Golf Course, Merrow

CATHEDRAL AND UNIVERSITY

CATHEDRAL AND UNIVERSITY

When the new diocese of Guildford was created in 1927 the initial plan was to use the town church of Holy Trinity as the Cathedral. It soon became clear that the church was too small for the expected congregation. So a competition was held for the design of a new cathedral. The design of Edward (later Sir Edward) Maufe beat the other 182 entries. Maufe wrote that his design should "rely on proportion, mass, volume and line rather than elaboration and ornament".

Building of the Cathedral started in 1933 on a six acre site on Stag Hil, donated by the Earl of Onslow. Work stopped at the outbreak of war in 1939. After the war a national shortage of building materials and a lack of funds meant that work proceeded very slowly. Then a fund raising drive from 1954 raised enough money to enable the Cathedral to be sufficiently completed for consecration in 1961. One fund raising scheme was the sale of bricks for two shillings and sixpence (12.5p) each. These bricks, which the purchaser could sign, were made of Stag Hill clay and would be used in the Cathedral building. The bricks signed by the Queen and Prince Phillip are displayed in the Cathedral.

The University of Surrey received its Royal Charter in September 1966, although its origins in Battersea date back to the 1890s. The University was built on Stag Hill next to the Cathedral, which acts as the hall for graduation ceremonies and other important events.

Academic buildings stand in the open setting of the Stag Hill campus. There are quiet corners for study and contemplation. One is Terry's pond (named after Terry Bennett, for many years the University's Head Groundsman), with its abundant waterfowl and the mirror-like sculpture of Narcissus by William Pye.

In April 2010 a world class Sports Park was opened on the University's second campus at Manor Farm, providing an international venue for many sports and an amenity for students and public.

The Cathedral stands out on the skyline and can be seen from miles around. Its tower is 160 feet high and has on top a 15 foot gilded Angel which turns in the wind. The Angel was given in memory of Reginald Adgey-Edgar of the Intelligence Corps, who died on active service on 5 January 1944.

Rose Window, Guildford Cathedral

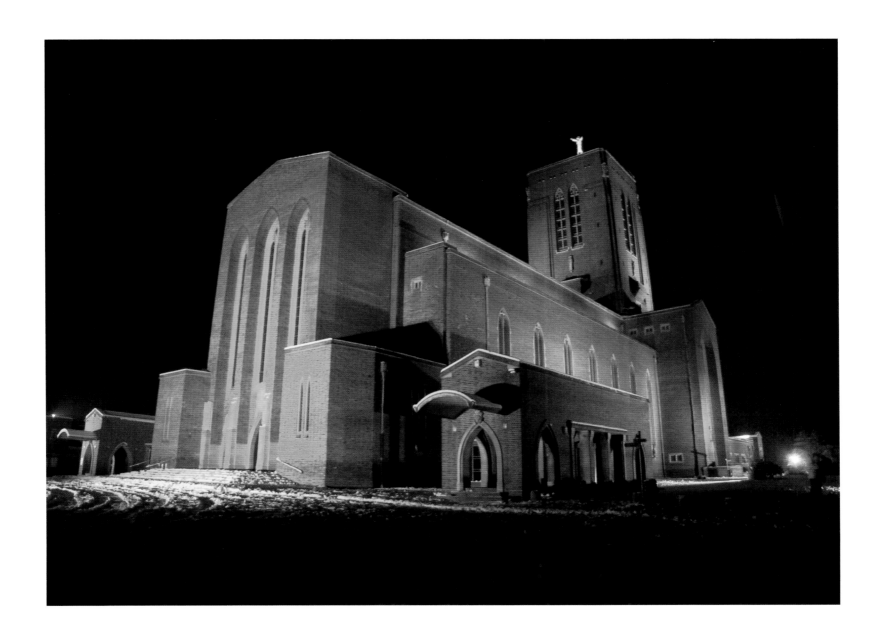

University of Surrey, campus view from Terry's Pond

'Narcissus', Sculpture by William Pye

Surrey Sports Park, University of Surrey

Guildford Cathedral >